Love Poetry and Songs
from
The Ancient Egyptians

by

Anonymous Royal Scribes
A Metrical Version

FOURTH EDITION

edited
by
Gilbert Moore

Original translations
by
Miriam Lichtheim
Bernard Mathieu, Richard Faulkner,
et. al

Blue Logic
ISBN 978-0-692-98470-3
2017

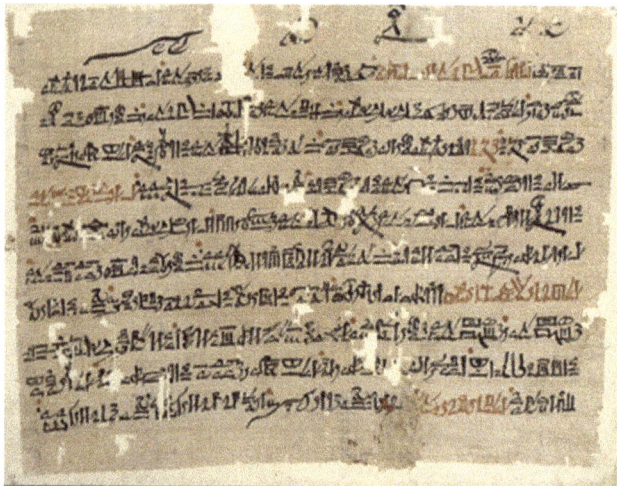

Ancient Egyptian hieroglyphs - HIERATIC SCRIPT-
circa 1300 BC -- 700 BC

PREFACE TO THE FOURTH EDITION

I

A confession: The compiler/editor of the original collection of love fragments assembled here never dreamed he would be publishing a preface to the fourth edition of this remarkable document because he never dreamed there would be a fourth edition. But Fate, being what it is and so full of surprises, evidently had other plans. So be it: A fourth edition, deserving most definitely a preface.

To begin with, why a fourth edition? Did I discover a new cache of love songs and poetry somewhere? Yes, but not nearly enough to justify another edition. What then? *A seismic shift in my own understanding of the Egyptian vision of love is why. I saw that drawing a sharp dividing line between secular and religious love poetry is pointless. Love poetry is love poetry.*

This revelation happened somewhere between the publication of the third edition in 2012 and this year's publication in 2017. I am recording it by publishing these additional love poems overlooked by being mis-classified.

What happened?

Dispairing of ever finding more than a handful, and nothing more, of those delightfully beautiful, fragmentary images of love in states of naive innocence written by a generation anonymous scribes during the dynasty of Ramses I and his descendants, I was suddenly prompted to look at this loss a different way. I opened and started turning the pages of Richard Faulkner's modern translation of the *Pyramid Texts* -- looking for I knew not what. I stumbled across it seconds after turning a few pages to look without knowing that was what I was looking for -- but stumbling across it and knowing I had found it: Ancient spells and incantations written in 2360 BC more than a thousand years before the generations of Ramses II to V, describing a higher, more noble emotional love, less instinctive and childish than the later Ramses' era love fragments.

The *Pyramid Texts* document the soul's journey into the afterworld for union with its Beloved, the aim being to re-generate itself and the Beloved thru this union.

Is this not love?

II

Included in this edition with other excerpts, Spells 141 and 142 of the *Pyramid Texts* tell us: *"There is no god who has become a star without a companion. Let me be your companion. O, look at me! You have seen the forms of the children of their fathers who know their spells and are now Imperishable Stars. May you see the two inhabitants of the Palace: Horus and Seth. May you spit on the face of Horus and remove his injury! May you catch the testicles of Seth and remove his mutilation!"*

And Incantation 221 evokes a Higher Love: *O Great One! O Great of Magic, O Flame-Uraeus! Inspire fear in the Soul as fear of You, ... inspire awe in the Soul as awe of You, inspire love in the Soul as love for You..*

This discovery opened the floodgates to finding love poetry everywhere in the ancient Egyptian teaching: To begin with, in plain view for nearly four years even in the first edition, the *Lamentations of Osiris* now appear in true light quite different from the other fragments. Far from being playful or disarmingly naive, The *Lamentations* are re-telling the story of the soul's grief over the loss of its higher states of presence in a song. Sung in two voices -- that of Isis and Nepthys -- the song is strangely hypnotic in its rhythmic invocation of the states of longing for presence and of presence itself:

> *Come to my house, your home, my house*
> *Come to me, the Enemy's not here.*
> *O Good Musician, come to my house,*
> *your home, my house, come and hold me.*
> *Come, play music on me. O do not leave me*
> *ever again.*

III

In the *Hymn to Osiris*, also included in this third edition, the love story of Isis and Osiris is retold, a third-person narrative, but this time also from the point of view of the soul itself, dying and passing into the afterworld:

THE SOUL: *What manner of land is this I have entered. It has no water or air; it is a depth that is unfathomably deep, a darkness darker than the darkest night, and men are wandering about aimlessly in it. Here a man cannot live in the quietness of the heart nor ever satisfy his longings for love. So let this be my aim: To let the Immortal One enter me instead of water, air, and longings for love, and to let quietness of the heart enter me instead of cakes and beer."*

Whose soul is this we hear for the first time? It is neither the voice of Isis, Nepthys nor Osiris nor the voice of a god at all, who are already immortal, but a new voice. Whose voice? It is the voice of the *human* soul, the soul of Ani, historically a deceased royal scribe who commissioned his colleagues to write the *Papyrus of Ani* for him before his own death. For the first time in the recorded human history we know anything about, humanity is documenting the soul's journey into the afterworld, its Journey Forth By Day. Written in the 14th century BC, more or less, at the same time as the *Lamentations* and love poetry of naive innocence and youth found in the Charles Beatty collection, the *Papyrus of Ani* records the impermanence of human life and everything infused with it, including love and suffering.

IV

And finally in the remarkably enigmatic *Book of the Two Ways, Part II* in its majestic closing, written circa 2130 BC, we witness the union of the soul with Osiris, celebrated shamelessly as sexual union:

CHORUS: The Gods have ordained the Great Soul of Osiris to come forth by day and copulate with Him. Speaking to our father Osiris each day, the Gods say: "Let Your Soul come forth and copulate with You.

THE GREAT SOUL: I am this Soul. I come forth by day and copulate with Osiris. He washes my mouth with the milk of the Red Cow, and I cross the sky, traversing the Light.

What then, is this true love in its highest form? Copulation of the soul and its orgasm with the God it is the soul of? And what gender soul? Male? Female? And what kind of copulation? Oral? Genital? *We do not know.* Is there a risk of distorting the message by taking it too literally? Maybe. Did the ancient royal scribe writing this cross a line we moderns dare not cross in religious writing? Definitely.

G. Moore,
November 4, 2017

INTRODUCTION

Appearances to the contrary, Humanity is blessed, and for three reasons: That it has any record of its Ancient Egyptian past at all, that we have been able to decode its fragmentary remains after centuries of ignorance, and that we have any traces of its 600-year, momentary fling with love poetry in its dying days. Going back perhaps tens of thousands of years, most of the records of the Ancient Civilization itself have been obliterated or, what amounts to the same thing, buried forever under Saharan Desert sand. And only owing to the genius of Champillion and the tireless efforts of six generations of Egyptologists since him do we now have a reasonably reliable decoding algorithm and dictionaries to slowly lift the veil of ignorance.

That any of the ancient love poems survived is a miracle. Equally amazing is the fact that out of thousands of years of writing the only love poetry to survive is confined to a narrow band of time: the 100 year Ramesside Period from The 13th to the 12 centuries. How is that even conceivable? Statistically it is improbable.[7]

[7] One commentator describes the remains: "There are three papyri with sets of long songs, and one fragmentary pottery jar covered in another set; in addition there are about twenty ostraca that bear compositions that have been identified as love songs (Mathieu 1996: 27, with list and reference to different opinions of modern commentators). The songs are written in the Late Egyptian phase of the Egyptian language, a formal version of the spoken language of New Kingdom Egypt. No Middle Egyptian equivalent survives, although parts of the Middle Egyptian composition now known as Kemyt seem to present a man justifying his absence to a grief-struck woman. There are no later manuscripts containing love songs...Perhaps the most elaborate series of songs is the cycle of seven stanze on the back of a

Two factors lessen the improbability: Either the Ramesside period was, in fact, the only period in which love poetry was ever written or -- which is a different way of saying the same thing -- there was something uniquely different about these 100 years permitting secular love poems to be written then and at no other time. One does not have to look far. It turns out these years 1300-1150 BC coincide with the reign of Ramses II and his immediate successors (Ramses III to Ramses V) when Ancient Egypt reached the zenith of her military and economic power before collapsing.

During this period a social class of well-educated secular royal scribes and temple craftsmen emerged rivaling the traditional priesthood in cultural influence, if not power. In their hands a new genre of literature appeared: Secular love poetry depicting in hieratic script real flesh-and-blood men and women, expressing real emotions and speaking to one another with real human feelings for the first time. Unfortunately, the state of affairs permitting this was to last only as long as the reigns of Ramses II and his immediate successors. Roughly 100 years.[8]

---

papyrus roll now preserved in the Chester Beatty Library and Gallery, Dublin (Papyrus Chester Beatty I, verso, column 1 to column 5, line 2: other love songs follow the cycle). In alternate stanze, a young man and a young woman sing of their love in separation. (Mathieu 1996: 26).

8   A stela has been discovered recently dating to about 700 BC. There is an inscription on it describing a woman named Mutirdis in terms resembling a love song from the reign of Ramses II and his successors 600 years before. This together with evidence from other written sources suggests the genre continued long after the Ramesside Period. (See Mathieu 1996: 36 n.34, 87 n.276).

The translations presented in this third edition represent the collective effort of at least three generations of Egyptologists, dating back to the late 19th century and reaching a highpoint in the translations of Miriam Lichtheim in the 1970s and the recent efforts of Bernard Mathieu and others.

Mathieu's contribution merits special recognition. Besides his translitertions, he gives us a structural overview, missing before, of the complete cycle of love songs (See *Seven Love Songs* below):

1. The Lover sings of his Beloved's beauty, and his wish to approach her.
2. His Beloved, separated, in the house of her mother, sings of her longing for his arrival.
3. The Lover abandons hope of reaching her
4. His Beloved struggles with her desires.
5. After seeing her, the Lover rejoices but is still separated.
6. After seeing him, his Beloved sings of her hope that her mother might share her sentiment.
7. Seven days of separation have left the Lover sick: only his Beloved can heal him.

Transliterations of these songs appear separately in *Appendix A.*

G. Moore
July 4, 2015

Seize the Day!

A Cycle of Seven Love Songs
from the Beatty Collection[1]
c.1550-1350 BC

I

This One, a sister without equal,[2]
 most radiant of all, she is
my morning star, rising and shining brighter
than all the others: Fair-skinned, almond-eyed,
her speech the sweetest of all, saying not
a word too much nor too little. Upright,
with firm glistening breasts, she has arms
like the finest gold, fingers like lotus
buds and hair like the purple-blue sky at dawn.
Thighs heavy-set with a narrow waist on legs
parading her mound of beauty, she treads
the earth with grace: With movements that turn
men's heads, she's captured my heart. A joy to me,
she 's the sun rising in my East! Come, see.

II

My brother's voice torments me, it makes me
sick with longing for him. He's next door at
his mother's house.[3] I hear him and cannot
go to him! My mother shouts: "Stop seeing
him!" Possessed by love for him, I can think of
no one else. How this thinking stings my heart!
Fool that he is, he knows nothing of this.
If he did, he would write to me. But am I
not the greater fool, knowing I want him
and saying nothing? Brother! I am promised
to you by the Gold of Hathor Herself.[4] Come
to me. Let me show Father and Mother
your beauty. They will rejoice, and everyone
will greet you with a shout: "Brother! Son!"

III

My heart has devised a way to see you.
I will go to your house and sit there
and gaze on your beauty. But going to
your house, I meet your Father Mehy sailing
home in his boat in the company of ten
young men. What will I do? Sail past?
But the Nile is a narrow road, there's no way
to hide my tracks, he is sure to see me.
Hiding my face I reveal my aim.
No, better to go to him and say: 'Here
I am, I am yours.' Then he will shout
my name and place me at the prow among
his followers, and there rounding the bend
of the river, I will see your face., dear friend!

IV

Like a wild bird banging against its cage,
my heart is beating frantically for
love of you, and if I saw you now,
it would surely fly from my mouth.
Pity me, dear brother, thinking of you,
I cannot slip on my dress nor wrap nor tie
my scarf. No purple-blue powder round
my eyes, no anointment with oil from
the Land of Gods.[5] "Go to him," my heart screams,
"Don't wait!" Foolish bird, be still. Brother's
coming, and all the eyes of both Houses will trail
behind him, winking. Heart, be still, I say!
Let no one say of me: "Poor girl, fell out
of his wagon, ravished, now a cracked pot."

V.

Praises to the House of Golden Horus,
I called to Hathor, she heard my prayer,
my mistress came to me trailing murmurs of
awe and respect from all the young men.
They call out behind her, "She goes to him!"
What strange miracle is this? She comes to me
as in a dream, she comes and whispers
"Awake, my love!" I awake and die from
too much love. She's not here! Today I
will give offerings of Thanksgiving,
fine fruits, nuts and palm seed oil. Elated,
exulting in my good fortune, I pray to
Hathor to send her. Four days pass,
five, now six. Come to me, I cannot last.

VI

Passing before his door again, I found
it ajar, this time looking inside I
saw him, mirror of my heart, my beloved,
standing next to his mother, and all
his brothers were there too. Love for him
has captured my heart. As I pass by,
he looks up and sees me. O, brother without
equal! Outstanding in virtue, you make
me tremble with joy. I know not where to turn,
I am beside myself with love. If only
your mother knew my heart, she would let me
enter. Golden One, let her heart know my heart,
then I will run to him, kissing him
on the mouth in front of every friend!

VII

Seven days without seeing sister,
and sickness invades me, my limbs grow heavy,
my body loses all sense of itself.
The chief physician comes to me, and my heart
finds no relief from his remedy,
and from ritual-readers, nothing.
They do not know the cause but I know:
Just telling me 'She is here' is my cure,
her name will raise me, the coming and going
of her messengers will cure me. Being
her brother is better for me than medicine:
better than prescriptions. Her visit is
the healing I need: Let her gaze on me,
and I will be well. Let her open her eyes
on me, and my body will be young again,
Let her speak, and I will be strong.
When we embrace, this sickness will go away.
My sister, gone now these seven days.

(Translators:M. Lichtheim (I-VI); B. Mathieu (VII))

Quatrains and Fragments[7]

A Song for Inherkhawy (fragment)

Seize the day! Celebrate!
Be tireless, and always in motion,
full of life -- you with your Beloved.
Let not your grieving heart
be sad today. As it passes by,
Seize the day!
> *circa 1539-1075 B.C.*
> (translated by JL Foster)

The Crossing (fragment)

I'll go down to the sea with you,
and come out of the water
carrying a red fish, just like so
in my hands.
> *circa 1350-1050 B.C.*
> (translated by MV Fox)

i

She knows so well how to cast the noose
and not pay the cattle tax. Caught by her
flowing hair, her soft eyes, and gold necklace,
with knees weakening, I lost the bill somewhere.

ii

Why argue with the heart. Go after her!
Embrace her. Kiss her on the mouth.
As Amun lives and gives me breath,[8]
Cloak over arm, I go.

iii

What she didn't do to me!
Why keep silent: She left me
standing at the door. Closed it in my face
 and walked away inside. Not even
a good night kiss!

iv.

Passing by her house in the dark,
I knock, no one opens the door.
No doorkeeper anywhere. Bolt, fly
open! Door, be my fate and show no strength.

v.

The door opened. Inside between
fine linen, lay a lovely girl.
She smiles and says: 'This is my house,
and its owner, the King's son, is coming.'

vi.

Riding the ferry north by the oarman's stroke,
I carry on my shoulder a bundle of reeds,
and in my heart a prayer: Ptah, Lord of
Truth, give me my sister tonight![9]

vii.

I lie down and pretend to be ill.
First the neighbors come, then the doctor,
Then my sister. She looks and tells them all
to go away. She understands my illness!

viii.

Caught by my bait, the wild goose makes a shrill
cry. My love for you is like that, and I
cannot loosen myself from my own trap. I go
to fetch the net. But what will I tell mother?

ix.

The wild goose breaks free and soars. Other birds
swooping down and swarming, greet him
in the air. But I? I am held fast by my love for you.
Tied to your heart, my heart has become the net.

x.

Brother, hearing you with half my hair
unbraided, I came at a run. Now look at me:
my hairdo neither this nor that! Wait, while I
unbraid the other half, then I'll be yours.

xi

Like honey plunging into scented oils,
your love penetrates me. Then like the pungent
smell of spices mixed with juice, escaping in thin air,
you run off with your sister! And I, left
behind a riderless horse grazing aimlessly
on the battlefield, a warrior rolling
on the axle of his broken wheels, no chariot.
Heaven made me love you, girl, not I:
I am the straw,   you the advancing flame,
and my longing: a hawk swooping down.
 O bird and flame, I am yours,
 consume all of me.

xii

Ripples in a pool of agitated water,
Concentric circles spreading outward,
disturbing rosebush and mulberry on
the shore. The rose is my sister's mouth,
its perfume her scented breasts. Her arms
an elusive mulberry bough, her face
the Moon of my delusions.
And I, the wild goose, the hunted one.
My gaze entangled in her hair,
I cannot loosen myself from her traps--
rose bush, bough, perfume, Moon.
I am caught. Now and forever.

xiii

This love-longing for you,
Is my heart not softened by it?
This dogfoot I wear, exciting
your passion, will I allow you
to remove it? No, not tonight.
Though beaten back to the Nile's
beginning, though beaten to Syria
with clubs and shebod-sticks, and to Kush
with palm-rods, though whipped to the highlands
with switches, and to the lowlands with twigs –
I will never, never abandon
my love-longing for you. Never.

xiv

I open the door to his bedroom,
and the morning bird sings:
"Come outside, day is returning,
the earth is full of light"
Quiet, foolish old bird! I go to brother.
He is there in bed asleep. I enter.

He wakes up. What joy! Happy beyond
words we embrace, vowing never
to part again. There in his bed,
my hand in his hand, his in mine,
the sun rising, the lark singing,
we begin wandering together to

distant and beautiful places. From that morning
I became his First Woman, and he never
grieved my heart.

xv

Beautiful Wife, let me rest my arm
for awhile on your arm.
Then I will go and fish and hunt
wild game for you.

Noble Husband, you have changed me forever
with your love. Waiting for you tonight, I said:
"Heart, be still". Return to me, my Lord,
I miss you so. Like the body in a tomb
missing its Soul, I need you.

My nets are cast, my quiver emptied.
Yearning for you, *dear wife,* I hurry home.
I have no knife to amputate
this love-longing from my heart. None.

The nearness of Your Presence delights me.
Your Being fills me with joy.
Like a sick man longing for his health
and strength to return, I hurry home,
longing for you.

xvi

Hearing your voice, dear brother, is like drinking
new wine.I long for the Sound of You, I become
intoxicated by it. And then to see you --
O, better even than eating or drinking.
Hearing your voice, your hand in my hand, , looking
into your eyes, my heart is a cup running
over with joy. I am drunk with love for you.

A breeze blowing from the North cools my face,
Water flowing through the deep canal
you dug cools our feet. I am your sister.
Like good dark earth in your hands I smell
of Nature's sweet perfume. Be careful though:
The *sa'am* [10]plant is in me too. Tasting me
you will soon be seeing double.

On the Other Side of the Nile

My sister waits for me with love
on the other side of the Nile.
But how am I to reach her?
Crocodiles are also waiting --
in the shallows. And out there midstream
the river will sweep me away. Roaring
past violently like lion herds, pounding
against its own banks, dissolving them
in loud crashes -- I can hear them --, the Nile
is swelling at floodtime. The Dog Star has risen.

But the thought of my Beloved strengthens me.
I brave the shallows, the crocodiles look,
then turn and swim away. They seem like mice
running from me. Unafraid, I walk upon
the rapids of the Nile swelling at floodtime.
Her love is a water-spell protecting me.

Now, standing on the other side, I look with love on my
Beloved. Smiling, she stands before me. We embrace,
then kiss, and like a Red Salmon jumping from its small
pond back into the sea, my heart leaps from my mouth,
entering hers as a kiss to join and become one
with her heart. Ecstasy of One Soul in two bodies,
we make love all night. O night, never end![11]
circa 1550-1050 BC

Stinking drunk (a fragment)

Fool, *ta-'a-ti* plants[12] were in it!
That's why you came home stinking drunk.
I will take off your garlands,
And when you are lying in bed
and I massage your feet,
And the children are in their...

The Saam-plant summons us[9]

The Saam-plant summons us:
I am your sister, the first and best:
Like this dark soil under our feet I belong to you.
Flowers and sweet-smelling herbs are planted here.

.

Sweet is the stream, dug by your hand,
Refreshing as the north wind.
What a lovely place to walk in,
Your hand in my hand,
My body next to yours, my heart
in ecstasy as we wander together;
Hearing your voice is like pomegranate wine,
I live for hearing it and tasting you.
Each look from you into my eyes sustains
 me more than food and drink.

Under Hathor's Protection

Come, my Soul, swim with me!
The water runs deep with my love for You.
Come, my Soul, to the middle of the water,
I hold and press flowers to my breast for You,
naked and dripping wet with water.
And the moon makes them glisten and bloom
like lotuses in the night.

Here, in the middle of the water of
my love for You, I give you these flowers
because they are beautiful and sweet.
And You take my hand, in the middle of the water,
holding and pressing me to You,
naked and dripping wet with love.

(Translated by J.M.Kellner)

O, my Soul, my lotus ...

O, my Soul, my lotus,
The north wind is blowing.
Let us go down to the river.
My heart longs to enter it
and bathe with You.
I will take off this robe of fine linen
to let You see my beauty
moist with balsam underneath.
My hair is plaited in braids of reeds
I enter the water to bath with you,
then leave it to join you on shore
With a little red fish I caught.
See it between my fingers,
 It is beautiful! I lay it down before You.
I look up and see your beauty.
O my joy, my lover! Look, see mine!
(*Translated by Hermann A. Schlögl in Gärten der Liebe ,
2000)*

Busy Old Bird, I hear you!

Busy old bird, I hear you! Awake now,
I must go. Dawn quickens into day.
But weary from a night of love-making,
where will I go? My Beloved is asleep
here beside me. I have nowhere else to go.
She stirs!
(source: http://www.perankhgroup.com/Ancient%20
Egyptian%20Love%20poetry.htm)

ii

Bird of Love, be quiet! I found true love
tonight, He is here beside me,
and I will go whereever he goes,
hand in hand with him always.
I am his flower, He my warming Light,
He told me so this very night.
(Translator:ziad@perankhgroup.com)

When I am not with you

When I am not with you,
where can I set my heart?
If I cannot embrace you,
where will I go?
(Translator: Anonymous)

How Well She Knows to Cast the Noose[10]

How well she knows to cast the noose,
And yet not pay the cattle tax!
She casts the noose on me with her hair,
She captures me with her eye;
She curbs me with her necklace,
and brands me with her seal ring.

Karnak at Dawn

*Come to My House, Your Home,
My House...*

Hymn To Osiris
(circa 1240 BC)

Homage to You, Osiris, Lord of Eternity,
King of the Gods, whose names are manifold,
whose forms are holy, You being of hidden form
 in the temples, whose Soul is holy...The stars in
the celestial heights are obedient to You,
and the great doors of the sky open themselves
before You. To You songs of praise are sung in
the Southern Sky, and thanksgivings offered
to You in the Northern Sky. Obeying You,
the Imperishable Stars are Your throne.

Your sister Isis protected You,
repulsing the fiends, and turning aside
the calamities of the Evil One. She uttered
the Spell disarming It with the Magic
of her mouth, her tongue being perfect,
without halting at a word. Isis, woman
of magical spells, looked for You
tirelessly, wandering the Earth in sorrow,
without finding You. Then Light out of feathers,
air out of wings, she uttered the death
wail for You and drew out of Your stilled heart
the still-flowing Semen, making of It
Horus and rearing Him in loneliness in
an unknown place. Your Son grew in strength
and stature, with a mighty Hand in the House
of Keb. And the Gods rejoiced at His Coming.

(*Journey Forth By Day, Papyrus of Ani* 1240 BC, translated by E.A.
Wallis Budge)

Out of the Light, the Holy Lotus
(circa 1240 BC)

THE SOUL: I am the holy lotus coming out of the Light of
Ra's Nostrils. I belong to Hathor's Head. I am making my
way to Osiris, seeking after Him in darkness.

Hail, Temu! What manner of land is this
I have entered. It has no water or air;
it is a depth unfathomably deep, a darkness
darker than the darkest night, and men
are wandering about aimlessly in it.
Here a man cannot live in the quietness
of the heart nor ever satisfy his longings
for love. So let this be my aim: To let
the Immortal One enter me instead of
water, air, and longings for love, and to let
quietness of the heart enter me
instead of cakes and beer.
(*Journey Forth By Day*)

Fragments from Lamentations for Osiris
(To be sung and danced)
c.1350 -1050 BC

ISIS: Come to my house, your home, my house
Come to me, the Enemy's not here.
O Good Musician, come to my house,
your home, my house, come and hold me.
Come, play music on me. O do not leave me
ever again. Come to my house, your home,
my house. Come to me, your mistress,
your sister, your wife. It's been too long,
Eternal Youth, too, too long since you held me.
My heart aches for you, my eyes shed
dry grief, no more tears. Come to my house,
your home, my house. Come to me, your sister,
your wife, the Enemy's fallen, the Enemy's not here.

NEPTHYS : Come, Good King, come to our house,
your home, our house. Come to my sister,
your wife, your heart. The Enemy's not here.
Good King, come to our house, your home,
our house. My Twin calls you. Hear her,
turn around and come. Drive away this pain
from our hearts. Dear Brother, come to our house,
your home, our house. Turn around and see us.
Come, Good King, the Enemy's fallen. Come.

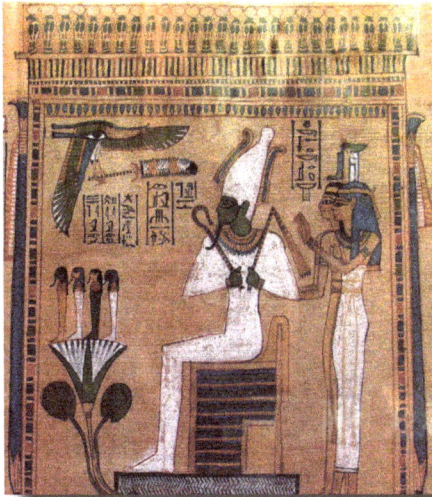

ISIS: You rise for us like the Sun at dawn,
Climbing above the Two Lands, you fill it with
Your Presence. The Evil One cannot enter.
Crossing the sky, you chase It away.
Your light warms Gods and men alike,
Protecting them. Even at night your Sacred
Image is with us – in The Child in the Moon,
in Orion among the stars. O, let me
be your dog star, and I will follow You
faithfully every night at your rising and setting.

NEPTHYS: O brother, O king, come to our house,
Your home, our house, come to my sister,
Your wife, your heart. Like a lusty bull,
come to her breasts full of love milk,
come, O brother, come.

The Great Soul of Osiris
(*circa 2181-2055 BC*)

THE GREAT SOUL: Doorkeeper of the narrow opening,
Let me pass! I am He Who Bruises
the Sides of the One Who Comes Out of
the Sacred Fire, I am He Who Kindles
Her Womb, I am the Great Soul of Osiris,
the Semen still flowing from His Phallus.

CHORUS: The Gods have ordained the Great Soul of
Osiris to come forth by day and
copulate with Him. Speaking to our father
Osiris each day, the Gods say: "Let Your Soul
come forth and copulate with You.

THE GREAT SOUL: I am this Soul. I come forth by day
and copulate with Osiris. He washes
my mouth with the milk of the Red Cow, and
I cross the sky, traversing the Light.

(*Book of the Two Ways "The Way of Eternal Life"* 2181-
2055BC translated by Richard Faulkner)

Pyramid Texts of Unas
(circa 2360 BC)

141: There is no god who has become a star without a companion. Shall I be your companion? Look at me! You have seen the forms of the children of their fathers who know their spells, who are now Imperishable Stars. May you see the two inhabitants of the Palace: Horus and Seth. 142: Spit on the face of Horus and remove his injury! Cattch the testicles of Seth and remove his mutilation!

Utterace 221 O Great One! O Great of Magic, O Flame-Uraeus! Inspire fear inUnas as fear of You... inspire awe in Unas as awe of You, inspire love in Unas as love for You....

Utterance 371. This Unas ravishes mankind as his (own) limb...Isis takes care of him, Nepthys suckles him,

372: Horus takes him to his side, he purifies this Unas in the Jackal-Lake, he cleans the Ka of this Unas in the Lake of Dwan, he rubs down the flesh of the ka of this Unas as well as his own...

378: May Unas love you, O Gods! Love him, O Gods!
(Source: http://www.pyramidtextsonline.com/sarcsouth.html)

379…. Horus climbs on the knees of Isis. Unas ascends on the knees of Nepthys…

381: Mother of Unas, Ipy, give to Unas this your breast, that Unas may pass it over his mouth, that he may suck this your clear sweet milk.

Appendix A Transliterations of
The Cycle of Seven Love Songs
(*Transliterations by B. Mathieu*)

Transliterated Title of the cycle:
HAt-a m rw nw tA sxmxt-ib aAt

Translation: Beginning of Incantations
for The Great Release

First Stanza

snt nn snw.s
nfr Hr-nb
ptri.s mi spdt xay
m HAt rnpt nfrt
Sspt iqrt wbxt inw
ant irty gmH
bnri spt.s mdwt
bn n.s xnw m HAw
qAt nHb wbxt qby
xsbd mAa Snw.s
gAb.s Hr iT nwb
Dbaw.s mi sSnw
bdS pHt.s mrw.t(i) Hr-ib
DA mnty.s nfrw.s
tw iwt xnd.s Hr tA
iT.s ib.i m Hpt.s
di.s st wn nHb TAy nb
msHn n mAA st
rSwt Hpty st nbt

sw mi tpy n mryw
ptr.ti pr.st r HA
mi tfyt wat

Second Stanza

Hwt snt
sn.i Hr stAH ib.i m xrw.f
di.f TAy n.i xAyt
sw m sAH-tA n pr n tAy.i mwt
nn rx.i Smt.n.f
nfrt mwt m Hn.i m nfy
i.xAa mAA st
mk ib.i HDn sxA.tw.f
iT wi mrwt.f
mk sw m iwty ib.f
iw swt iw.i mi qd.f
bw rx.f nAy.i Aby Hpt.f
mtw.f hAb n tAy.i mwt
sn hAy tw.i wD.kwi xr.k
in nwb Hmwt
mi n.i mAA nfrw.k
rSwt it mwt
nhm n.k rmT.i nbt m bw wa
nhm.sn n.k sn

Third Stanza

Hwt xmtnwt
xmt ib.i r mAA nfrw.s
iw.i Hms.kwi m-Xnw.s
gm.i mHy Hr Htr Hr wAt
Hna nAy.f mryw
bw rx.i iT.i m-bAH.f
snny.i Hr.f m wstn
ptr itrw mi wAt
nn rx st rdwy.i
xm.t ib.i r iqr
wstn.k mHy Hr ix
mk ir snny.i m-bAH.f
iw.i Dd n.f pXrw.i
mk iw.i n.k kA.n.f
iw.f swhA m rn.i
iw.f Hr dni.i r tA kpy tpy
nty imyw-xt.f

Fourth Stanza

Hwt fdnwt
ifd sw ib.i As
Dr sxA mrwt.k
bw dd.f Sm.i mi rmT
sw tfy mk.tw.f
bw dd.f TAy.i mssy
bw wnx.i pAy.i bhn
bw dd sDmw r irt.i
bw wrH wi m kfA
m ir aHa pH.t Xn
xr.f n.i r tnw sxA sw
m ir n.i pAy.i HAty wxAy
i.ir.k xAniw Hr ix
Hms qbH iw n.k snt
irt.i qnw m mitt
m rdit Dd nA rmT r.i
st tw hA tw m mry
smn.ti r tnw sxA.k sw
ib.i im.k ifdy

Fifth Stanza

Hwt diwnwt
dwA.i nwb sSwA.i Hm.s
sqAy.i nbt pt
iry.i iAwt n HwtHr
Hknw n Hnwt
smi.i n.s sDm.s sprw.i
wD.s n.i Hnwt
sw iAy.ti Hr Ds.s r mAA.i
aAyt wsy xprw n.i
Haw.kwi xntS.kwi wr.kwi
Dr Dd yH mk sw
mk iAy.s mry m ksy
n aA mrwt.s
iry.i smAaw n tAy.i nTrt
di.s n.i snt m diy
hrw xmt r sf Dr sDm spr.i
Hr rnw.s pr.s m-a.i Hr hrw diw

Sixth Stanza

Hwt siwnwt
swA.n.f m hAw n pr.f
gm.i aA.f wn
sn aHa r-gswy mwt.f
snw.f nb r-Hna.f
mrwt.f Hr iT ib n xnd nb Hr wAt
sfy iqr nn mitt.f
sn stp biAt
gmH.f r.i m-Dr snny.n.i
tw.i wa.kwi r nhmw
xntS wy ib.i m TAHw
sn Dr mAA.i
hAn mwt rx.ti ib.i
iw.s aq.ti n.s r nw
nwb hAy imi sw m ib.s
kA Hnw.i n sn
snny sw m-bAH nAy.f iryw
bw Tmw.i n rmT
rSwt.i n pAy.sn aAmw
r-Dd tw.k rx wi
iry.i Hbw n tAy.i nTrt
tf ib.i r pr
r rdit gmH.i sn m pA grH nfr
wsy m swA

Seventh Stanza

Hwt sfxnwt

sfx r sf bw mAA.i snt

aq aq n.i xAyt im.i

xpr.kwi Haw.i wdn

smx Dt.i Ds.i

ir iw n.i nA wrw swnw

bw hr ib.i pXrt.sn

nA Xryw-Hb bn wAt im.sn

bw wDa tAy.i xAyt

pA Dd n.i mk sw pA nty sanx

rn.s pA nty Ts.i

pA aq pr n nAy.s wpwtyw

pA nty sanx ib.i

Ax n.i sn r pXrt nbt

wr sw n.i r tA dmdyt

pAy.i wDA pAy.s aq r-bnr

ptr.s kA snb

wn.s irt.s rnpy Haw.i

mdt.s kA rwd.i

iw.i Hpt.s sHr.s Dwt Hr.i

pr.s m-a.i Hr hrw sfx

ENDNOTES

1   Source: Miriam Lichtheim, *Ancient Egyptian Literature*, vol. II (University of Calif. Press, 1976)

2   [1] The hieroglyph for *sister* and *brother* consists of a two-barbed arrowhead -- the same kernel except for the determinant, a female for sister, male for brother. The two-barbed arrowhead image literally means 'two' as in 'twin', 'couple' and 'duality'. Transliterated, *snt* for sister, *sn* for brother, it also means 'my double', 'my other half' (Gardiner, 514).

3   The hieroglyph for *mother* is an example of the Ancient Egyptian enjoyment of punning. Transliterated as *mut*, the vulture hieroglyph for mother is the same as the hieroglyph for the Egyptian female principal of maternal love and respect, not sexual excitement (in contrast to Hathor). See below.

4   *Hathor*, representing the Egyptian female principle of sexual excitement and longing, literally means 'House of The One Who Cuts His Enemy to Pieces'. She was also called "The Golden One".

5   More than likely referred to here, frankincense was a perfumed oil used by ancient Egyptian woman to anoint themselves. The oil came from Punt, the exact location of which is unknown, but may have been Southeast Egypt (perhaps Nubia or Southwest Arabia). Punt is often referred to as *ta netjer*, 'Land of Gods'

6   Miriam Lichtheim, *Ancient Egyptian Literature*, vol. III

7   Miriam Lichtheim, *Ibid.*, vol. II

8   A reference to the Sun God in his hidden aspect, the name *Amun* means 'hidden one or 'secret one'.

9   The hieroglyph for *Ptah*, the Egyptian principle of creation (the humanity, pottery, engraving, metal work), is punned openly here: It is the same as the hieroglyph for *prayer*

10   *Sa-am* a plant, possibly a sexual stimulant, cited by EAW Budge in *Egyptian Hierogylphic Dictionary* and classified parasitic by him, properties unknown.

11   From IIIa. Miriam Lichtheim, A Collection, The Cairo Vase 1266 + 25218 and George A. Barton, *Archaeology and The Bible*,

3rd Ed., (Philadelphia: American Sunday School, 1920), pp. 413-416. Written perhaps during Egypt's New Kingdom (1539-1075 B.C.) but more than likely composed even earlier, these love poems were found in the excavated ruins of a workers' village on the outskirts of the Valley of Kings.

12   *Ta-ti* could be a reference to a plant grown in soil fertilized with the Egyptian crocodile excrement *tit*

13.   In this context, *saa(m)* has two, related meanings: a literal one denoting a seed or fruit used in medicine, and more than likely by lovers as a sexual stimulant. Also, it turns out, *Saa* is a hieroglyph for the ancient Egyptin God of Knowledge and Intelligence. (Budge, vol. II, p. 641) Translation download: http://www.humanistictexts. org/egyptlov.htm from 1-9 Ancient Egyptian Literature—A Book of Readings, Volume II: The New Kingdom, translated by Miriam Lichtheim. The University of California Press, Berkeley, California, 1976. pages 182-193.

14.   source: http://www.perankhgroup.com/Ancient%20 Egyptian%20Love%20poetry.htm

http://bluelogic.us

www.ingramcontent.com/pod-product-compliance
Lightning Source LLC
Chambersburg PA
CBHW040803150426
42811CB00082B/2379/J